Art In History

Ancient Chinese Art

Jane Shuter

www.heinemann.co.uk/library
Visit our website to find out more information about Heinemann Library books.

To order:
☎ Phone 44 (0) 1865 888112
🖹 Send a fax to 44 (0) 1865 314091
💻 Visit the Heinemann bookshop at www.heinemann.co.uk/library to browse our catalogue and order online.

First published in Great Britain by Heinemann Library, Halley Court, Jordan Hill, Oxford OX2 8EJ, part of Harcourt Education.

Heinemann is a registered trademark of Harcourt Education Ltd.

© Harcourt Education Ltd 1997, 2006

Editorial: Clare Lewis
Design: Victoria Bevan, Michelle Lisseter, and Q2A Media
Illustrations: Oxford Illustrators
Picture Research: Erica Newbery
Production: Helen McCreath

Printed and bound in Hong Kong by WKT

10 digit ISBN 0 431 05667 6
13 digit ISBN 978 0 431 05667 8

10 09 08 07 06
10 9 8 7 6 5 4 3 2 1

British Library Cataloguing in Publication Data
Shuter, Jane
Art in History: Ancient Chinese Art – 2nd edition
709'.5'1'0901
A full catalogue record for this book is available from the British Library.

Acknowledgements
The publishers would like to thank the following for permission to reproduce photographs:
© Art Archive/British Library, p. **12**; © Art Archive/National Palace Museum Taiwan/Harper Collins Publishers, p.**19**; © Art Resource, p.**7**; © Art Resource/Werner Forman Archive, p.**9**; © Art Resource/Werner Forman Archive, p.**27**; © Art Resource/Werner Forman Archive, Idemitsu Museum of Art, Tokyo, p.**8**; © Art Resource/Werner Forman Archive, National Palace Museum, Taipei, p.**13**; © The Bridgeman Art Library Int'l. Ltd. (U.S.)/Private Collection, p.**18**; © Corbis/Burstein Collection, pp.**11, 25**; © Corbis/Ric Ergenbright, p.**28**; © Corbis/Kimbell Art Museum, p.**10**; © Corbis/Lowell Georgia, p.**20**; © Courtesy of Cultural Relics Publishing House, pp.**4, 5, 22, 23**; © The Granger Collection, p.**6**; © Idemitsu Museum of Arts, p.**24**; © National Geographic Image Collection/O. Louis Mazzatenta, pp.**16, 17**; © Nelson-Atkins Museum/The Nelson-Atkins Museum of Art, Kansas City, Missouri (Purchase; Nelson Trust) Photography by Robert Newcombe, p.**29**; © NHK (Japan Broadcasting Corporation) & NHK Publishing, p.**26**; © Science Museum of London, Science & Society/Picture Collection, p.**14**.

Cover picture of Yellow Emporer Huang Di, reproduced with permission of Uniphoto Japan/Ancient Art and Architecture Collection.

Every effort has been made to contact copyright holders of any material reproduced in this book. Any omissions will be rectified in subsequent printings if notice is given to the publishers.

The paper used to print this book comes from sustainable resources.

Contents

Some words are shown in bold, **like this**.
You can find out what they mean by looking in the glossary.

WHAT IS ANCIENT CHINESE ART?

Ancient Chinese art was created between 1500 BC, when China began to be ruled by royal families called **dynasties**, and AD 1279, when the **Mongols** conquered China. This covers almost 3,000 years of art, in a country just a little larger than the size of the United States today. It takes hours to move from one side of China to the other by aeroplane, but in ancient Chinese times people walked or rode animals and went much more slowly. Few people travelled over large distances, so Chinese art developed differently in different parts of the country.

Most of the ancient Chinese art that we have comes from the periods nearest in time to our own. Almost all of the early examples of ancient Chinese art we have are of **bronze** pieces, because they survive best. This does not mean bronze work was the only art produced at this time.

This is the first early bronze to be found that shows a human figure. It was found with several heads made in a similar style. The first reaction of many people to these heads is how "un-Chinese" they look—the style did not stay a part of Chinese art for long. We do not know the names of any of the artists of this period.

Bronze figure, Sanxingdui, Central China, c. 1200 BC, almost 1.8m (6ft) high without base. With the base it is over 2.7m (9ft).

How artists worked

Almost all ancient Chinese art before AD 1000 was made for a particular person, called a **patron**, who ordered a specific piece. Artists did not create beautiful things and then look for a buyer because materials were too expensive. This did not just apply to painters. Weavers, bronze workers, and carvers all worked in the same way. An artist's best chance of earning a good living was to get work from rich, important people. Emperors set up workshops for weavers, bronze makers, and carvers, and regularly ordered paintings from favoured artists. From the time of the Tang dynasty, a style of court art developed. Painting on **silk** scrolls became popular. Painting and **calligraphy** became fashionable pastimes for important people. Many of the nobles at court, and even the emperors themselves, were artists.

Beaker, ivory inlaid with turquoise, c. 1200 BC, 30cm (12in) high

Elephants lived in China at the time this beaker was made, so ivory was a local material. The turquoise was a trade item from far away. The beaker was made for the **tomb** of the Shang dynasty queen Fu Hao, who was buried in 1200 BC. It is one of the few surviving pieces of early Chinese art that s not made from bronze. It shows that there were early artists with other skills, though much of their work has not survived.

MATERIALS

Chinese art, to us, includes many things the ancient Chinese did not see as art, such as pottery bowls. The Ancient Chinese thought that making things like bowls, screens, and statues, was a craft skill. They did value beautiful things made by craftsmen, and Emperors set up workshops where crafts could be made for the court. However, to the ancient Chinese, artists were people who produced paintings, poetry, and calligraphy. These skills were called "the three perfections".
Writing was a very important art – both writing the Chinese characters well, and writing a poem to match the feeling in a painting.

The carefully placed red seals in this painting give the names of various owners of the painting. The seals were not seen as spoiling the picture, but adding to its worth by showing how many important people had liked it enough to buy it.

Landscape, Ts'ao Chih-po, ink on silk, c. AD 1260

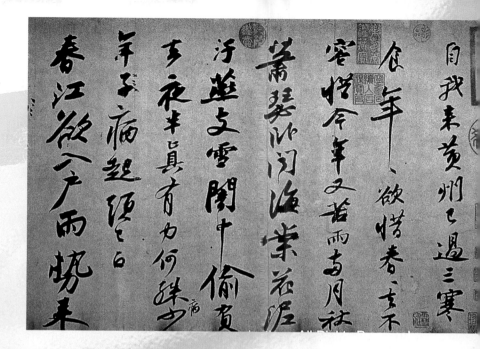

Poem, ink on paper, Song dynasty, c. AD 960–1279

The artist and poet who wrote this poem in calligraphy used different parts of his brush to make the thick, heavy lines and very thin lines in the characters.

Artists' palette

Chinese artists painted with water-based paints and ink. Various natural substances and **pigments** were mixed with water to make paint colours: powdered clamshells made white; red ochre, a kind of earth, made brown; and some artists even used real silver and gold. Ink was made by mixing soot (black smut from burning wood, coal, oil, or even hair and bones) with glue to make a hard cake. To make ink the artists had to grind off a little of the ink cake, very finely, and mix it with water. Many artists painted only in ink. They thought that the type of soot used and the amount of water added made such differences to the tone of black that there was no need for any other colour. Artists used brushes made from animal hair that came to a very fine point at the tip. This meant they could make very thin lines.

Making your mark

Many early works of art had inscriptions saying who the people in the pictures were. Later, the artists also signed them. Because most art was made to order, the owner of a painting was important. Many pieces of Chinese art are stamped with the seals of their owners. With some pieces of art you can discover how they passed from owner to owner from when they were first painted to the present day.

ART AND RELIGION

There were three religions in ancient China: **Taoism**, Confucianism, and **Buddhism**. Most of the time they were all accepted, and they all had an important place in ancient Chinese art. A lot of art was made for religious reasons: to be buried in tombs, or to decorate tombs and temples. Before 400 BC, emperors and other important people had real people buried with them in their tombs, to serve them after death. This was because ancient Chinese beliefs about life after death included taking servants and possessions with you into the next world. After 400 BC, the human sacrifices were replaced by terracotta, **earthenware**, or **stoneware** figures of servants, animals, houses, and entertainers. Tombs and temples were both decorated with wall paintings or carvings. Temples were also decorated on the inside and outside with large statues of important religious figures.

Musician, terracotta, Han dynasty, 206 BC – AD 220

This statue is a model of a musician, made to be put into the tomb of an important person. This statue shows us how musicians looked and performed in ancient China.

Buddha, rock carving, Yungang caves,
Wei Dynasty, c. AD 460–494

The Yungang caves have some of the earliest
examples of Buddhist art that exist in China.
They were not destroyed in AD 843 because
the caves are hidden on high cliffs.

Reproductions of famous art

In AD 843 there was a brief time when Buddhists were **persecuted**
in ancient China. Temples, with their beautiful statues and wall
paintings, were destroyed. A Tang dynasty writer, called Zhang
Yanyuan, was shocked by the loss of the works of art. He decided
to make the first art reproduction books, called *Records of Famous
Paintings of All the Dynasties*. They had careful reproductions of
famous works of art in them, as well as stories about the lives of
the artists who painted them and a discussion of various styles of
painting. These books contain the only examples of many ancient
Chinese artists' work that have survived.

PAINTING: LANDSCAPE AND STILL LIFE

The ancient Chinese painted on various surfaces. At first, they painted on walls, wood or, less often, on silk. From 300 BC, silk scrolls became the most common surface to paint on. It was not until after AD 1000 that paper was widely used. Both paper and silk were first treated with an **alum** wash, to stop the ink from **bleeding** too much. Chinese artists, unlike western ones, painted the **foreground** first and then worked back, doing the background last. Once they were dry, paintings were given another coat of alum to set the colours.

The Song dynasty painter, Guo Xi, said "landscape paintings must show a harmonious relationship between earth and heaven." The ancient Chinese wanted their paintings to show nature, but nature controlled and in order, not nature as it appeared around them. Early landscape painters put people or buildings in the landscape, but they were very small. The most harmonious landscape would show both earth and water, because this produced a balance of the earth and water elements.

Landscape in the style of Tung Yuan, by Wen Chia, ink on paper, c. AD 1577, 167cm x 52cm (65¾in x 20½in)

The artist of this landscape copied the techniques used in the Song dynasty. It follows the rules written by Xie He.

Painting of Bamboo, painting on silk, Yuan Dynasty, c. AD 1260–1368

The patron who commissioned this painting wanted people who saw it to think he was a strong person. The ancient Chinese audience would understand that the bamboo in the picture was a symbol of strength as well as a beautiful image.

Many things used in landscape and still-life painting were **symbolic**. Snow symbolized purity, bamboo showed strength, and plum blossom showed simplicity. Dragons were not supposed to be frightening, as they are in many western cultures. To the ancient Chinese they symbolized strength, wisdom, luck, and goodness.

The six rules of painting

The ancient Chinese developed rules for painting. Of course, no one had to follow them, but the most admired paintings were the ones that followed these rules. The rules were outlined by Xie He in about AD 500:

1. The painting must have vitality.
2. The brush must be used properly.
3. The painting must show accurately what is painted.
4. The right colours must be used in the right order.
5. Things must be arranged harmoniously in the painting.
6. A painter should learn the art by copying. When you copy a painting make sure it is accurate, in the spirit of the first painting, and respectful of the first painter.

PAINTING: PEOPLE AND ANIMALS

Ancient Chinese artists favoured calm, still scenes. Frantic movement and violent emotions were seen as things that quickly passed and that were not admirable. Even when they painted busy town scenes, or crowds of people in motion, there is still a feeling of calm in ancient Chinese pictures, and a sense that every person in them is going about his or her business in an organized and purposeful way. There is a sense of order and control, just like there is in the landscape paintings.

Portrait of Empress Wu Zeitan, the wife of Emperor Gaozong Tang, painting on silk, 18th-century copy of a painting from c. AD 705

Wu Zeitan was the first Empress of China. She lived from AD 624 to 705 AD. This picture was probably used for **ancestor** worship, an important ceremony for the ancient Chinese.

Accurate images

When painting people and animals, the ancient Chinese did not try, like the ancient Egyptians, to show a perfect version of that person or animal. They wanted to make an accurate picture that would capture the spirit of the person or animal. The artist who painted Empress Wu Zeitan included her wrinkles to make the picture accurate.

Gu Kaizhi

Zhang Yanyuan called Gu Kaizhi "the father of Chinese painting" in his illustrated book of Chinese art in AD 847. Gu lived from about AD 345 to AD 406. During his life, he had been considered an important artist by some people, but his fame increased after his death. By the time of the Tang dynasty, when Zhang was writing, Gu was widely respected and his paintings were frequently copied. Gu was important because, while he used traditional subjects and poses for his paintings, he used a more realistic style than earlier artists. His animals and people seem alive, and are often painted as though the artist caught them just as they were about to do something. By Tang times Gu was being given almost sole credit for the move towards accurately representing subjects in a painting.

It looks like the **groom** has just pulled the rein on the horse he is riding, causing it to turn and look at the viewer, while the horse in the foreground turns to see why the other horse moved. These kinds of realistic reactions are examples of Gu's innovative realistic style.

Two Horses and a Groom, *painting on silk,* c. AD 700–800

BRONZES

Bronze working is seen as one of the earliest forms of Chinese art. This is mainly because it is almost the only form of art to survive from earliest times to the present day. The first bronze workers made large, heavy bronze pieces for use in burials. The important thing about these seems to have been that they were big, imposing, and beautifully decorated. At first, the various royal dynasties seem to have controlled bronze making. It is possible that bronze pieces were seen as something that only important people should possess. Bronze was used to make big, heavily decorated objects at first. Later bronze workers made much more delicate objects. Some of these smaller objects were simply decorative, but some were useful, too.

Earthquake detector, made by Chang Heng, bronze, c. AD 132

Each dragon's head on the jar has a ball in its mouth. The shaking of an earthquake made the ball drop from the mouth of the dragon on the side of the machine farthest from the centre of the earthquake into the mouth of the frog below.

The Lost Wax Method

The lost wax method of making bronze let ancient Chinese artists make whole objects covered in a lot of detail. These are the stages:

1. First, the artist made a wax model of his work. This could be very simple, with smooth flowing lines, or very detailed.

2. The artist covered the finished model in a thick layer of wet clay, leaving a large hole at the top and several small holes at the bottom. The clay was left to dry.

3. When the artist was certain the clay was dry, he heated up the clay. As the heat worked through to the centre, the wax melted and trickled out of the holes at the bottom of the clay mould.

4. Once all the wax was out of the mould, the artist plugged the hole in the bottom of the clay mould. He then poured in melted bronze. Because the bronze was runny, it filled in all the spaces left by the wax.

5. The artist left the mould while the bronze set, then broke it open and took out the finished bronze.

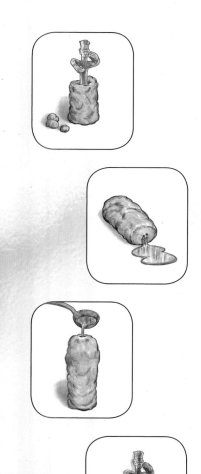

Using bronze as glue

Early bronzes were made in pieces, which were then carefully joined together, using freshly heated bronze as glue. Each piece was made by pouring melted bronze between two clay pieces. One piece was smooth, to produce the smooth inside of the bronze piece. The other side had the pattern of the bronze made in it, but reversed so where the clay pattern went out, the bronze pattern went in. From 500 BC onwards, bronze workers began to use the lost wax method of making bronze pieces. They could make even more beautiful and complicated pieces using this method.

TERRACOTTA

Terracotta is made from clay mixed with water, then moulded and baked at around 900 ° C (1,652 ° F) – three times hotter than the hottest setting on your kitchen oven! Terracotta was used mainly for simple things such as everyday pottery or roof tiles. It was also used to make models of houses, animals, and people to bury in tombs. Most of these models were small. However, some important people were buried with life-size models. In 1974, **archaeologists** were working near the mound where the emperor Sui Huangdi, of the Qin dynasty, is buried. They found a pit containing the first soldiers of a life-size terracotta army. The pits are still being **excavated**, but archaeologists think there are 7,000 soldiers in all. The group of people who made them would have included artists to produce moulds; workmen to make the pieces; builders to make and repair the kilns used to bake the warriors; metalworkers to make the weapons; and a huge army of workers to collect and deliver the firewood that was needed to keep the kilns running.

Archer, terracotta,
Terracotta Army of Sui Huangdi,
c. 210 BC

This life-size archer's hands are empty, but when he was made he would have been holding real arrows and a real bow. All the terracotta warriors were armed with real weapons. Tomb robbers stole many of these soon after the emperor was buried. Some of those that were left behind must have been treated with something to prevent rusting. They are still shiny and sharp after more than 2,000 years.

In this picture it is possible to see both the way the warriors were mass-produced and the ways they were individualized.

Mass production

One of the most interesting things about the Terracotta Army is that it is one of the earliest examples of **mass-produced** art. There were a limited number of parts, which were joined in various combinations. For example, for the standing warriors, which were about 1.8 m (6 ft) tall, there were three styles of plinth for the warriors to stand on, two different styles of pairs of legs, eight different body shapes, two different types of arms, with hands made separately, several styles of hand, with the fingers made separately and put together in different combinations, and eight different heads. The features and hairstyles on these heads were then worked on by hand, to make the soldiers look less mass produced.

POTTERY

Chinese potters made beautiful bowls, jars, plates, and other objects from earliest times. They divided their pottery into two main types: earthenware, which was **fired** at 800°C (1,470° F) and pottery that was baked at a much higher temperature. Westerners came to divide Chinese pottery into three types: earthenware, stoneware, and **porcelain**. Earthenware is pottery fired at a high temperature that is any colour from black to grey inside, and porcelain is pottery fired at such a high temperature that it is pure white inside. Westerners valued porcelain highly, because they did not know what was added to the clay to make it white when fired. This made porcelain very valuable to the Chinese as a trade item.

Camel tomb model, earthenware, c. AD 618–906

The ancient Chinese used camels a lot for carrying goods on long trips. During the Tang dynasty, tomb models became more carefully detailed and glazed. They were used in more tombs too, not just the tombs of important people. Most pottery sculptures were made of earthenware, stoneware, or terracotta, because they were less expensive than porcelain.

What made porcelain special?

Porcelain was especially hard and smooth, as well as white. It could be made much thinner than other pottery, too. Good porcelain was very thin. In AD 851 a visitor called Suliman, from the Middle East, remarked, "The Chinese have a fine clay which they make into vessels equal in quality to glass, for you can see the liquid they hold inside them." The ingredients that gave porcelain its special qualities were a white clay, called kaolin, mixed with a rock called petuntse. Petuntse was also powdered and added to the glaze used to coat porcelain. It made the glaze harden quickly and also made it harder to chip. Porcelain was traded widely, and was a very valuable material in China and in the West.

Ju porcelain, Song dynasty, c. AD 1086–1106

Porcelain made in the kilns at Ju is rare now. It was made for just 20 years, between AD 1086 and 1106. All of the porcelain made there was made for the **imperial** court.

The secret of porcelain

Europeans discovered the secret of porcelain by accident. Johann Bottger, a young man who said he thought he knew how to turn metal into gold, had been put in prison by Augustus II, King of Poland. Augustus wanted to know the secret if Bottger found it. Instead, while firing earth at high temperatures, Bottger discovered porcelain. He was put in charge of the first European porcelain factory in Meissen, Germany.

RELIEF CARVING

The ancient Chinese made carved stone slabs, intended mainly to go on tomb walls or on the walls of **shrines** to important people. Carvers began to work in stone when the tombs of important people began to have public areas where visitors could come, probably to pay their respects to the dead person buried or remembered there. These carvings are called **reliefs**. They are carved so that the design is raised from the background. The carvers used similar scenes over and over, and modern Chinese historians think that they are intended to link ideas about the afterlife to ideas about social order on earth. So a battle scene would show both a battle on earth, symbolic of social disorder, and show chaos and order battling for the dead person's soul in the afterlife.

Rubbing of a stone slab relief, from the Shrine of Wu Ban, Jiaxing, northeast China, c. AD 147

A whole series of shrines devoted to the important Wu family were built at Jiaxing. No one was ever buried at the shrines, but the carvers used the same ideas and images as they did for tomb carvings. They also carved images of everyday life, like this one, that we can use to find out about what the ancient Chinese looked like and how they dressed.

Make your own wall relief

Stone carving took a long time and could be very expensive. Brick reliefs were also made to decorate stone walls. The design was drawn up and marked into brick-sized rectangles. Moulds were made to stamp the design onto each brick. The bricks were then fired one by one, and built up to make the original design.

Materials:

- **cardboard**
- **pencil**
- **scissors**
- **string**
- **glue**
- **ruler**
- **modelling clay**

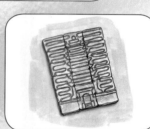

1. Take a piece of card 30cm by 30cm (12in by 12in). Draw a design on it. Keep it simple the first time!

2. Mark the design into bricks 7.6cm by 5cm (3in by 2in).

3. Glue string to the parts of the design that you want to be the background. You may need to mark your brick lines over the string in places. Leave your wall to dry.

4. Cut carefully along the brick-marking lines.

5. Number the back of each piece of card, so you know where it goes in the picture.

6. Make 24 bricks 7.6cm by 5cm (3in by 2in) out of modelling clay.

7. Use your card bricks to print your design onto the clay bricks. Keep your matching clay brick and your numbered card brick together.

8. Build your wall, using the numbers on the card bricks as a guide.

JADE AND LACQUER

Ancient Chinese artists made beautiful objects with lacquer and jade from the earliest times. In both cases, the work was difficult and time consuming.

Jade is an extremely hard stone. There were two types of jade, nephrite and jadeite. Neither could be found in China, so they had to be traded with other countries. Nephrite was the most valued kind of jade. It came in green, brown, beige, and white. All jade was so hard that it could not be carved the way other stones were carved. Jade workers had to use very strong tools to make a rough shape and then do the actual carving by rubbing the shape with a powdered mineral called quartzite. The rubbing process took much longer than ordinary carving. Even a simple bracelet could take days.

Immortal on horseback, white jade, c. 70 BC, 9cm long and 7cm high (3½in long and 2¾in high)

White jade was the most beautiful of all jade to the ancient Chinese. This carving shows a mythical figure on horseback. It comes from the tomb of the Han emperor, Zhaodi, who died in about 70 BC.

Lacquer working

Lacquer is made from the sap of the lacquer tree, a relative of the poison ivy plant. The sap is drained off and can be coloured with various pigments and used like paint or varnish. It can be painted onto various surfaces, including wood, baskets, and stone. When dry, it is heat and water resistant and very shiny. This makes it practical. It is also very beautiful, especially when colours are built up in many layers to produce pictures that have a lot of depth. Each coat of lacquer takes about two days to dry. Some of the most beautiful pieces of lacquer work, made for emperors and very expensive, can have as many as 200 coats of lacquer. Lacquer artists had to be very careful workers. Mistakes on any of the layers could ruin the whole piece.

Screen, wood and lacquer,
c. 484 AD, 79cm (2ft 7in) high

This screen is from the tomb of Sima Jinlong. The Sima family was an important family in northern China. The pictures on the screen are copies of silk scroll paintings by Gu Kaizhi. At this time, everyone sat on cushions or mats on the floor. So the screen, which was a room divider, only needed to be about a metre high.

CALLIGRAPHY

Ancient Chinese writing began as picture writing. Each picture stood for a particular object, action, or emotion. These pictures are much more recognizable in very early pieces of writing–the character for a house really looks like one. As time passed and people wrote more, they changed the characters and five main calligraphy types developed:

1. *Zhuan shu*, the first written language to be used all over China, was developed in 221 BC by the First Emperor. It stayed in use on the seals that the ancient Chinese used as personal signatures.

2. *Li shu* was developed in about AD 200, during the Han dynasty, for record keeping.

3. *Kai shu* was developed in about AD 250 for ordinary writing. It is the most common writing today, and is the script used for printed books.

4. *Xing shu* was developed in about AD 300 as artistic writing. This is the writing that was used with paintings and was considered an art form.

5. *Cao shu* was developed in about AD 650 for making notes. It is the quickest to write, but the least beautiful.

Mountain Market in a Clearing Mist, *Yujian, ink on paper, c.* AD *1250*

This painting was made by the Buddhist **monk** Yujian. The writing on it is a poem in xing shu writing.

Five-coloured Parakeet on a Branch of Apricot Blossom,
Emperor Hui Tsung, painting on silk, c. AD *1100–1135*

This painting includes a calligraphy poem.
The artist has painted the calligraphy
characters as carefully and perfectly as
the image of the parakeet.

Perfect characters

Ancient Chinese calligraphy was seen as an art form because the aim
was to get each character perfect, which was very hard to do. You
had to hold your brush in the right way, load it with just the right
amount of ink, make the brush strokes in the right direction, and
keep each brush stroke for each character in proportion with all the
others. Each character had to be copied over and over again. The
Chinese still try to make perfect characters today. Many art stores sell
Chinese brushes, inks, and books that show how to paint the various
characters. Some libraries have the books, too. It takes a great deal of
patience and copying to get even simple brush strokes just right.

TEMPLES

From the earliest times the ancient Chinese believed in spirits and demons that could affect everyday life. They also believed in ancestor worship, because they thought the spirits of their ancestors could affect everyday life. Emperors and their ancestors were worshipped, too. Religion and everyday behaviour were linked together, and Chinese families had shrines in their homes where they could worship. They also built temples where monks and other people could gather to meditate and worship. Many temples were built in caves. They were beautifully decorated, inside and out. There were huge carvings of spirits, demons, and teachers. They were linked to both Buddhism and Taoism.

The 11 colours used to decorate this cave have been analyzed, and they include expensive mineral pigments from far away. The artists who painted them were craftsmen employed by the state, who were not allowed to work for anyone else. Their work was probably passed down from father to son. They worked constantly in the complex of caves, repairing crumbling stone and renewing the paint.

Paintings in the Mogao Caves, Dunhuang, China, c. AD 538. This is the interior of cave number 285.

Qiyun "Cloud Reaching" Pagoda, Luoyang, China, c. AD 1175

Pagodas were a form of Buddhist temple with roofs in many storeys. The number of storeys on a pagoda is based on numbers that were important in the Buddhist religion. Pagodas did not replace cave temples. They were built when a tall and graceful temple was more suitable for the landscape.

Shrines

Shrines were places of worship and meditation that were smaller than temples. They were often dedicated to ancestors of important families. In some cases, like the Wu shrines in Jianxing, there were several shrines to different members of the same important family. In other cases, a shrine was built for one particular member of a royal family, who was seen as being especially powerful and having a large influence on everyday life. An example of this is a shrine to the Sage Mother, an early Zhou empress. It was beautifully decorated and had a huge painted statue of the Sage Mother and several small statues of ladies-in-waiting. As well as being worshipped as an ancestor, the Sage Mother was worshipped as a goddess who could bring rain. Shrines did not have artists working full-time to keep them going like temples did. Artists were brought in when there was work to do.

BUILDINGS

The ancient Chinese built beautiful homes and gardens.
The various emperors and their families had the most beautiful
homes. Their palaces were built inside high walls and were
huge, with courtyards, gardens, and lakes. From the time of
the First Emperor onwards, emperors also had various large
building projects, such as roads, canals and, most famous of
all, the Great Wall.

*The Great Wall of China, c. AD 1350,
about 2,700 km (1,678 miles) long*

The Great Wall was built with various materials, depending on what the builders
could find in each local area. Much of the wall was made with packed earth that
sometimes had layers of reeds packed in too, to absorb moisture. In the Gobi
desert, local plants and sand or stones were used; in other places, builders used
logs and clay. In all cases, the materials had to be solidly packed down before the
builders added the next layer.

Tower house tomb model, stoneware, c. 206 BC – AD 221

This tomb model shows a walled tower house and its courtyard and main gates. Many homes were only one storey and stretched away from the main entrance. Tower houses were built in cities with many people, where space was a problem. From the model you can see that artists carved and painted the outside walls of the houses, as well as the inside walls and the gates.

Homes

There are no imperial palaces still standing from the ancient Chinese period, although some have been **excavated**. There are no accurate paintings either. Imperial palaces were private, since the royal family did not want people to know how they lived. This created a custom of keeping homes private that was soon followed by all people, from emperors to city tradesmen. Most homes had a central space open to the sky, which they called the "well of heaven". In the homes of wealthy families there were several courtyards. The farther away from the main double gates you went, the more private the parts of the house were. Homes were built using wood, and roofs were covered with terracotta tiles. Inside spaces were divided up by screens that were often beautifully carved, lacquered, or painted.

TIMELINE

BC

1766–1122	The Shang dynasty rules China.
c. 1400	Artists begin bronze working in China.
c. 1300	Writing begins to be used in China.
c. 1200	Queen Fu Hao is buried.
	Painting on plaster walls begins.
	The Sanxingdui bronzes are made.
1122–480	The Zhou dynasty rules China.
	Many large bronze objects are found in burials of this time.
551–479	Confucius lives and teaches in China.
c. 300	Silk is first used as a painting and writing surface.
480–221	The Warring States period. During this time different parts of China are ruled by different dynasties, and it is not united.
221–206	The Qin dynasty rules China.
c. 220	Writing is standardized across China by the First Emperor.
c. 201	A terracotta army is made for the tomb of the First Emperor.
	The first Great Wall of China is built around this time.
206	The Han dynasty begins to rule China.

AD

220	The Han dynasty ends its rule of China.
c. 100	Paper is invented by the Chinese.
c. 100	Buddhism becomes an important religion in China.
220–581	Various dynasties. During this time different parts of China are ruled by different dynasties, and it is not united.
c. 345–c. 406	Gu Kaizhi lives and works in China.
c. 500	Xie He writes the Six Laws of Painting.
538/539	The earliest dated painted temple cave is completed at Dunhuang.
	Trade with the West via the Silk Road allows westerners to appreciate Chinese art.
581–618	The Sui dynasty rules China.
c. 600	Porcelain is invented and perfected in China.
618–907	The Tang dynasty rules China.
845–847	Buddhism is temporarily persecuted, and much art is destroyed.
847	Zhang Yanyuan produces books with pictures of the art of the great artists.
907–960	Five Dynasties. During this time different parts of China are ruled by different dynasties, and it is not united.
960–1279	The Song Dynasty rules China.
984	The emperor sets up an official Imperial Painting Academy.
c. 1000	Paper is first used as a painting surface.

GLOSSARY

alum powder made of chemicals and minerals that can be sprinkled over ink or paint to dry it

ancestor someone who lived before you in your family, like a grandparent

archaeologist person who studies the past by looking at monuments and artifacts of certain cultures

bleeding when ink blots on a surface and looks fuzzy

bronze metal that is a mixture of copper and tin

Buddhism religion based on the teachings of the Buddha

calligraphy writing made with artistic lettering

dynasty kings and queens in the same family

earthenware pottery fired at low temperatures that cannot hold water unless it is glazed

excavated uncovered by an archaeologist

fire bake clay to make it able to hold water

foreground part of painting that looks like it is in front of the picture

groom person who is employed to take care of someone's horses

immortal thing that lives forever

imperial having to do with the emperor

mass-produced a lot of things made at once that look exactly the same

Mongol person from Mongolia, a country that was next to China

monk man who gives up his job and family to devote his life to religion

patron person who orders art

persecute to harass people because of their religious beliefs

pigment coloured material taken from animals, plants, earth, or rocks, and used to make paint or dye

porcelain pottery made from kaolin and petuntse and fired at a high temperature

relief carving with some figures raised to stand out from the surface

shrine place that is dedicated to a religious figure and used for worship

silk cloth made of the material that silkworms make to build cocoons

stoneware pottery fired at high temperatures that can hold water

symbolic when a picture of something suggests a bigger idea

Taoism religion based on the ideas of Lao-tzu combined with the ideas of Buddha

tomb place where dead people are buried, often elaborately decorated

FIND OUT MORE

You can find out more about Ancient Chinese art in books and on the Internet. Use a search engine such as www.yahooligans.com to search for information. A search for the words "Chinese art" will bring back lots of results, but it may be difficult to find the information you want. Try refining your search to look for some of the art and ideas mentioned in this book, such as "terracotta army" or "calligraphy".

More books to read

Anderson, Dale. *History in Art: Ancient China*. Oxford, Raintree, 2005

Hibbert, Clare. *World Art and Culture: Chinese*. Oxford, Raintree, 2006

INDEX